Through My 8-Yr-Old Eyes
BOOK 2
(Back to Pine Bluff)

THROUGH MY 8-YR-OLD EYES (BOOK 2)
Copyright © 2022 by Debora Cole Dockett

Published in the United States of America

ISBN   Paperback: 978-1-957312-76-7
ISBN   eBook: 978-1-957312-77-4

All rights reserved. No part of this publication may be reproduced, stored in a retrieval system or transmitted in any way by any means, electronic, mechanical, photocopy, recording or otherwise without the prior permission of the author except as provided by USA copyright law.

The opinions expressed by the author are not necessarily those of ReadersMagnet, LLC.

ReadersMagnet, LLC
10620 Treena Street, Suite 230 | San Diego, California, 92131 USA
1.619. 354. 2643 | www.readersmagnet.com

Book design copyright © 2022 by ReadersMagnet, LLC. All rights reserved.

Cover design by Kent Gabutin
Interior design by Dorothy Lee

Through My 8-Yr-Old Eyes

BOOK 2

(Back to Pine Bluff)

DEBORA COLE DOCKETT

ReadersMagnet, LLC

I remember running home one rainy Friday evening when we lived in SlotPot. The rain had caused the road to be icky with thick red mud which made it hard to walk. One of my shoes got stuck in the mud and as I stepped, it was pulled from my foot which plunged into a puddle of cold muddy water.
The hood on my raincoat flipped over my eyes when I leaned over, causing my satchel to slide over my shoulder, which fell into the water then splashed onto the part of my face that wasn't covered. I started whining to myself,
"Hmm!! Make me sick, old stupid bag!!!"
What made it worse, was that dat-gum Boo-Boo.
I promise you I don't know where she came from but… she came out of nowhere trying to ride a tricycle in the mud and, yes!! Knocked me face first into the mud.
As usual, she had that jaw full of tobacco, had on a rain scarf and her feet and socks were soaked.
"Boo-Boo!! You crazy thang what's wrong with you!!!!"
  She was laughing her behind off.
"You already wet so what!!"

When I stood up, I held onto the back of her tricycle so she couldn't ride off.

Then I started laughing and she got mad.

"Git yo han' offa my bike."

"It ain't a bike it's a trike!"

"Let it go!"

I grinned.

"Okay."

So, I let go as she pulled. And she along with her tricycle tumbled into the mud. She got up crying as I ran home.

The last thing I heard her yell, was *"Fool."*.

That was the last time I saw Boo-Boo. While I was struggling with mud issues, other action was taking place inside the house. I don't actually remember what happened among the adults, all I know is that when I stepped inside, my mom had two great big bundles of our belongings tied up in sheets. Because of the look she had on her face, I knew this was a time to shut up and just listen.

The babies were bundled and ready to go as she sat on the bed with her pocketbook beside her. My sister stepped up behind me as I was going into the house. Momma didn't waste any time with details.

"Sandra Kay!", she said.

"Uh-oh!", I thought. *"First and middle name!"*

My sister just stopped and looked at her.

"Go get that boy down the street and ask him would he take us to Pine Bluff!"

"Now?" Sandra asked. Her face lit up.

"Right now!!" Momma demanded.

"Tell him I'll give him 20.00!"

"I think my sister was out of that door before Momma finished that sentence."

In the 60's, twenty dollars was quite a bit of money for a teenager. Anyway, the old uncle was standing between the makeshift pasteboard door just looking. I think he and Momma had a bad argument while we were at school. She was tired of living like a caveman and said, *"Enough is enough."*. We couldn't have agreed more. Talk being happy!!! We were so ready to come back to our home—the home that we knew. My stepfather came through the door and just started grabbing things and tossing them out in the car when our ride pulled up five minutes later. We were sitting on things and things were thrown to us, at us, on us. We didn't care.

We just knew we were going back home!!!

Back to Pine Bluff!!!!!
As we rode, the rain came down harder and harder. Our driver had to go slower because the wind from the thunderstorm almost made his windshield wipers stop. My sister was so happy that she was smiling and talking all the way…Totally different than when we reached Slot Pot. My Aunt and Uncle were not expecting us, but they were happy that we had returned home -- Looking a pure mess!! Later on, I found out through general conversation we looked like Granny 'nem from THE BEVERLY HILLBILLIES!
Probably even worse. You wonder why I say that?
I will tell you why.

Let's see, where do I start? Before we left Pine Bluff, we were cuties. I had nice length hair and was your regular sized 8 -year- old. My aunt and uncle took very
good care of my sister and me. I always said that she was my second mom (and I still say that) My sister Sandra adored our aunt. We were the daughters she never had. But as I said she loved us dearly and she showed how much through the way she cared for us.

When we showed up at that door, she hardly recognized us. My Mom was down to a size 6 from a sized 16. All her hair had come out from the cotton poison that came from the crop dusters as they would drop right in front of our house to spray the cotton crop. I don't know what caused this last thing to happen, but every evening between the hours of 3 to 6 her hands would start stinging and then they would itch and break out with large welts. We would grab the alcohol and she would wash her hands, and it would disappear until the next time but my mom never complained. I knew she was tired of that life.

As a child, all I could do was just to shower her with hugs and kisses and tell her I loved her.

Sandra didn't lose much weight, but her face was a mess. She had large lumpy, bumpy knots and white heads. One of the teacher's embarrassed her by squeezing them in front of others and talking about why our mom didn't take her to a doctor– something she did not mention until later and refuse to talk about afterwards. She hated Slot Pot so badly that once we left there, she never ever wanted to talk about it. It was a terrible, terrible time for her. She was growing up and that place was no place for someone coming of age. Memories? That place probably gave her nightmares!!! Didn't have to worry about the babies. Everybody did whatever it took to keep them safe. As for me? I probably looked worst of all. I was already, small but I got even smaller. Because of the cotton poison, Sores developed in the sides of my mouth, and I was unable to eat because it hurt. We had no money, so we did the home remedy thing. Gargle with warm salty water.

As we begin to settle in, I felt like I was dreaming!! That little six room home felt like a mansion. The rooms were spacious, and we could use actual electricity instead lamps and candlelight!!! My cousins looked us in dismay.

"*Wow!*", said my cousin who was about a year older than I was. He took his index finger and his thumb and encircled my arm and there was still space enough to put something else.

"*Wow!*" He said again.

"*Ma, Look!*"

Then he closed his hand up around my wrist. My Aunt just looked and shook her head and sighed.

"*You want something to eat?*"

I was too excited to eat, but my uncle had already fixed us a plate... All of us. Just our luck they were having hamburgers.

Well, not so lucky for me. I couldn't eat. That very day my aunt and uncle begin to take charge of the situation. My Uncle took one look into my mouth and said a grown person's word.

"*Jean, come look at this!!*"

My aunt, momma, stepfather and everybody was staring in my mouth with the ugliest frowns on their faces. I became alarmed when my sister exclaimed, "*Eww! That's nasty!*"

My little cousin was looking and said, "*Why her jaws bloody?*"

I started to cry, because that was the first time, I heard the term "blood" being used. "*What you cryin' about? Stop crying. I'm gone fix you up.*", said my uncle.

For a period of time after that day my uncle would swab my mouth with peroxide. I would rinse and when I had finished doing that, he would take a Q-tip and gently swab the inside of my cheeks with a tiny bit of Iodine. Thank goodness for his skills as a paramedic when he was in the military. My aunt looked at our hair and said that she wanted to break out in tears when she looked us.

My two healthy ponytails were two little nubs of hair. My own clothes had gotten too large. They just couldn't believe what had happened to at us after leaving Pine Bluff, but we were back and now we could start the healing process.

I awoke the next morning to the smell of breakfast. My nose picked up aromas of coffee, cocoa, bacon and you could hear the eggs frying. We all begin to stir, stretch and yawn. The guys slept *"Hey, Y'all better get up."*, summoned my uncle goes behind my sister and me.

On a sleeper sofa and they had placed a comfortable mattress on the floor for my sister and me. There was no room for lagging and (as the grown-ups would say), Lolly-Gagging around because Saturdays were for cleaning and boy, that day was super busy! We had to find places to put the things that we brought along with us. Anyway, Uncle came and stood at the door to raw-hide us into moving along. The boys got dressed first. (You know how it is.)

They only have a couple of pieces to put on, take a quick personal time and then here it comes.

Uncle comes in with a small white homemade apron around his pants, wiping his hands on a towel, slings it over his shoulder then takes a seat on the edge of the couch and calls the boys to him and do his Saturday routine.

"Wash your face?"

"Yes Sir."
"Brush your teeth?"
"Yes Sir."
"Comb your hair?"
"Yes Sir."
He turns to the older cousin and says, *"Are you sure you combed your hair?"*
"Yes Sir!"
"Go get me that comb!"
Wayne comes back with the comb; Uncle gets it and begins to go back over his hair. Poor Wayne's head looked like a turtle ducking in and out of his shell. He didn't say anything. He'd just duck and bob. Edward, on the other hand was a different story.
"Ow! Daddy!! That hurt! Ouch!! Daddy!!!!!!"
Then he begins to cry. Unlike Wayne who only ducked his head, Edward weaved and bobbed like a boxer. Uncle would sometimes take the comb and give him a few taps on the shoulder. (Only taps). But you would think he had beat him down.
"Stop all that cryin'."
The more he combed Edward's hair, the louder he got. When he finally finished combing, tears, drool and snot was everywhere.
And just as suddenly as he started crying, he stopped when Uncle dragged the comb through his hair the last time.
"Now go wash your face again and get ready to eat.", said Uncle.
I thought that was it over and then he turned to me.
"You need to go put your clothes on and tell your Momma to do something with yo' hair."
I was a little surprised.
"Why is he fussing at me?", I thought.
"I'm gonna comb my own hair."

I got up from bed and scooted on into the bathroom. Mom and Aunt Dorothy later explained to me, that since we shared a room with boys, I had to be more careful of what I did. I didn't think too much of what I did in front of them. I was eight years old!!

After taking care of business, breakfast was next. Although my mouth was sore, I tried to eat, but I could only eat just a little bit. Cocoa gave me discomfort, but I drank it anyway.

Uncle took care of my mouth again that morning. Once breakfast was finished, the real work began. Gathering dishes and dumping leftover food. We had to heat dishwater to wash dishes, sweep the floor then mop it. Since it had rained the night before, it was too muddy outside to do yard work, so we helped with storing things, filling spaces that were unused. Luckily there was a dresser in the other bedroom. It was filled with things Mom had, the babies, things and her husband's things. As a matter of fact, the room they were in held all our belongings. Heck, we didn't have much at all. Once we finished, then and only then we could watch TV or go outside. Things had settled down and normal times begin.

We had been back in Pine Bluff for about 3-weeks, and it certainly felt like we were in the right place. I loved our house. It was a 6-room home with enough love and space for everyone. Even if I wanted to be in my own little world, I could find my own little corner with a stack of books to read. Most of the time though, Edward and I would be playing somewhere or outside. I forgot to mention that it was in the middle of the semester. When we came back it was a little before Christmas break. There was a decorated tree and lights and of course presents under the tree …none of which belonged to us. Due to our situation this was the first time I did not get anything for Christmas. I was a little sad -- not much. I held fast to the thought that maybe, just maybe something would be placed under that tree for me. Every now and then when I got the chance I would sneak and look through the presents to see if I had anything. I never gave up hope. Decorations and food still made the holiday feelings come through. But my wonderful Aunt Dorothy always had a trick or two under her sleeve. There were a couple of dolls in storage that had been put away when she and her sister, Earselean had gotten to the age where their dolls had probably started being more for bed decoration than for play.

I get chills all over right now as I think how Uncle pulled down the old, dusty box. He and Aunt Dorothy started coughing and sneezing as they used dust rags to remove the dust. She pulled out a large soft doll whose arms and legs would make a sound when you squeezed them. She was in perfect shape. The perfect doll to sleep with. She had on a little white gown with a white bonnet. The doll my sister had was a porcelain doll with a soft body. When you would hold her forward and then lean her backward, she would say *"Ma-Ma"*. I was s-o-o happy You would have thought old Santa himself had personally handed the present to me. That Christmas was just as good as all the rest.

As a matter of fact, it was better than the rest. A gift I had no idea I would get, food, fruit, fun and family, not to mention other people's toys. I felt like I was in Christmas heaven!!!! It didn't take very much to make me happy!! As the days passed, we continued to get reacquainted. Some nights we sat and listened to Mom and Aunt Dorothy catch up and talk about some of the happenings. Both had interesting things to say. Some I better keep to myself. I can tell you about the *"Rabbits and Squirrels"* though.

At one point in Slot Pot, work for my stepfather was non-existent. He worked construction and that year was a very, very rainy year which meant no work. He loved to hunt with a passion, so we had to live like people lived in the true olden days. Anyway, he taught my sister how to use a .22 rifle. She was only 11 but she became a marksman. He and she would go into those woods and kill rabbits and squirrels, and rabbits and squirrels and more rabbits and squirrels! At first it was different eating that type of meat because we had always eaten regular meat. Chicken, pork chops sometimes steak. I remember the first time When he bought home a few rabbits that they had killed. I could not believe it. *"You killed Bugs Bunny and his family!!"*
"Who?", he asked.
"Bugs Bunny?"
"Who dat?"
My sister stepped into the conversation.
"He's on the cartoons."
"Is?"
I nodded my head while I stared at the dead rabbits on the floor.
"Well, I reckon him and his family gon' taste pretty good, yeah ah'm gon' eat 'em. deep fried with some gravy and rice and biscuits! You betta have some !!"
"Uh-Uh!!!! I don't want to eat no dead rabbit!!!"
"You don't know what you missin' ", he said as he slashed the rabbit's head off.
When he slit the rabbit I said," What *you do that for?"*
"I gotta git his guts out, Chile!"
When he pulled the insides out, my stomach balled up and I ran into the house. Once all the preparing was done, he handed the rabbit

over to Mom and she worked her magic and it did smell pretty good, but I still refused to eat it. Day after day rabbits and squirrels. The day came when I finally decided to try it.

I first spat it out. I just couldn't bear the thought of eating Bugs Bunny, but the day came when I gave in. I would eat the rice and gravy and a couple of bites. Still couldn't get past the wild taste. But anyway, rabbit and squirrel rabbit and squirrel.

My sister and I added to the conversation.

"When someone asked us what we had for breakfast?"

"Ra-a-b-i-t"

"What did we have for lunch?"

"Ra-a -b-i-t"

"What did you have for dinner?"

"Ra-a-b-i-t!"

"What did you have for dessert?"

"Ra-a-b-i-t!"

"What did you have as a snack?"

"Ra-a-b-i-t!"

First rabbit, then squirrel. When he skinned the squirrel, I could not believe It when my sister asked for the squirrel's tail.

"What you gonna do with that?"

"Probably put it on a stick."

"For what?"

"I don't kno……Hey! I got a idea."

"What? What you gone do?"

She didn't say a word. She grabbed her pants and somehow attached the tail to the back. She was always doing something strange. I'll say one thing, after that day, we knew we were not the only ones who ate wild life!

Not only was a squirrel tail attached to her pants, I begin to see squirrel tail hats, squirrel tail shoe tassels, squirrel tails attached to note books and even squirrels' tails on teen antennas. I guess you could say, that's the only time you were allowed to play with your food. We all laughed a while. It was good to see mom laugh again. Not only was my aunt her sister, they were best friends. We were now at the time where attention was put on getting everything right for school. My dress was starched and ironed. It was an old-fashioned dress, but it was a dress I liked very much. In Slot Pot, the people had no problem with it, but Pine Bluff kids? I will get into that in a minute.

My dress was a little bit on the long side. It was a red straight dress with a white collar and white cuffs with little green checkered boxes scattered over the dress. Mom had bought me a pair of brown suede tennis shoes with pointed toes. I loved them and I couldn't wait to wear them. I would take them out of the box and try them on every time someone would ask what kind of shoes did I get. The night before we would have to go to school, I could barely sleep. I kept thinking about the shoes, the new school supplies, and my favorite dress. When Mom washed and ironed the dress, it looked as good as new. My hair had been washed and my little ponytails had been crossed and pinned across my head. I looked pretty decent. At least I thought I did. I was so excited to start the next day, I don't even remember going to sleep.

"Y'all get up! Time for school!" Everybody was excited to get back to school. The boys were ready to continue the semester, and I was ready for a new start. My sister could care less but, she slowly did what she needed to do. No matter where she was, always the last one to do whatever was at hand. I rushed to put on my dress. Mom prepared my lunch. Two peanut butter sandwiches and 3 cents for a carton

of milk. I took the brown paper bag and stuffed it into my satchel. We all had cereal for breakfast. We gobbled it down and headed to the bus stop. Ralph walked ahead, Edward started to run *but* Aunt Dorothy warned him.

"Edward Charles! Don't run out in that street!!"

"Wayne watch that boy!"

"Yes ma'am."

We started out of the yard on our way to the bus stop. I started getting nervous as we got closer to the stop. There were more kids there than I thought it would be, and I felt those critical stares and sneers.

As we arrived. I took my place beside a tree. My excitement began to dwindle when I encountered some of the kids. Particularly Rodney and Nita. My heart begins to beat fast. They walked over to me, looked me up and down Then they begin to sniggle. They walked about a few feet away and begin whispering.

"Hey girl, whut yo' name"?

"Debora Cole", I said.

Trouble was brewing. I could feel it. Nita walked back over to Rodney, whispered in his ear and the two of them begin laughing so loudly that they attracted the attention of the others. My favorite cousin was ignoring what was happening. Nita came back over and looked directly in my face.

"Hey girl, why you so ugly?", she said.

"Yeah, why you so black?", added Rodney.

"Y'all so crazy!", said another girl.

"OOooh, Y'all need to be shame!", said a girl. Then she burst out in laughter.

By this time, my eyes were full of tears. *"Cry baby! Cry baby! Nah na-na-na-naaah-nah."*, said Nita.

"Nita, come over here! ", said Rodney. She went over to him and he whispered into her ear and she begin to giggle.

"Ooh! Boy!"

He took small steps all the way to me, turned his back to me and started sounding like a screeching car and scratched dirt all over my new shoes.

"Oh, uh, you got dirt on your new shoes!"

"Them some ugly shoes.", said Nita. Again, they laugh. They left me alone for a minute. Then they started running by and hitting me in my back. I didn't know what to do. I thought my cousin would help me. All he said was, *"Hit 'em back."* And he and Edward ascended onto the bus. I cried softly. My happy day was turning into a horror day. All I wanted to do was to go to school and make new friends. When I got onto the bus, it was so full that we had to stand near the front. The best part of that was we had to stand near the bus driver. He must have been strict because everyone was talking softly and the bullies had stopped pushing and hitting, but that didn't stop them from making faces and licking out their tongues at me. But I didn't care about that.

When the bus let those two out on their side of the campus, I breathed a sigh of relief. Little did I know that my troubles were just beginning. As we climbed from the bus, my cousin had boarded first so he had to come from the back. We had been told that Wayne would help me get into a class. He was a kid too, so naturally his attention span was not what the adults thought it would be. He led me to his previous year's teacher, Mrs. Taylor. Told me to sit in a seat, and that was the last of him. Lucky for me, my half-sister was in that class.

She saw me and said, *"Debora!"*

We gave each other a hug.

"What you doin' here?"

"Comin' to school, but I don't know where to go."

The bell rang and everyone suddenly scrambled to their chairs. I was sitting in someone's seat.

"Mrs. Taylor, this girl is in my s-e-a-t!! I can't sit d-o-w-n!"

Mrs. Taylor Frowned and softly said, *"Don't be rude! "*

"Come here baby." I went to her desk, and I begin to cry again because I didn't know what to do.

"What's your name?"

"Debora Cole.", I sniffled.

Then my sister spoke up. *"That's my sister."*

"Who brought you here?"

"My cousin."

"Who is your cousin?"

Then Sherry interrupted. *"He brought her to this class.",* she said.

I had an envelope in my hand that had my report card in it. I gave it to Mrs. Taylor. she told me to have a seat then went across the hallway. I watched as she talked to this pretty but not-too-friendly-looking teacher. I heard Mrs. Taylor say,

"But what are we going to do with her?"

Then I heard the other teacher say, *"I guess I'll take her."*

Sherry had given me the run down on the class and the teacher. I was hoping that I would get to stay in this class. Mrs. Taylor called me to the door and as she escorted me to the other class, Sherry asked,

"Mrs. Taylor, can she stay in here? Please?"

She gave a sweet smile.

"No, I'm sorry. I don't have enough space."

I had a lump in my throat. First day of the new semester I was dropped off like a bag of potatoes, had been bullied by people I had never seen, rejected out of one class. What next?

The teachers decided I would go to Mrs. Virginia Williams class. When I stepped into the class, she did one of the things I hated the most— Class introduction.

"Class say hello to our new classmate, Debora Cole."

They all gave a half-hearted, *"Hey Debora Cole."* Some put their heads down and you could hear them sniggling. I heard someone say under their breath, *"She ain't new."*

Mrs. Williams walked over and stood over one of the boys.

"What is so funny, Lennard?"

"Nothin'."

She gave him the evil eye for a minute until he settled down. As I looked around the classroom there were two groups of students.

One group looked like your average everyday kids, with a few new outfits, maybe fancy sneakers and the other group looked like kids who were down and out, some smelled, one was sucking a thumb and others just looked like they were mad at the world. That was the group I was placed in. She took one look at me and placed me in the group with remedial students and she had no idea of what level I was on.

"Cole, where are you from?"

I was ashamed to say the name of the town.

"Did you hear me?", she asked as she looked over her glasses.

"Slot Pot.", I mumbled.

"Speak up, can't you talk?", she said in an irritated tone of voice.

The students laughed.

"Slot Pot!" I almost yelled.

She looked up at me again. A girl from the "smart" group, glared at me side-eyed and quickly cut her smile.

"Is everybody as ugly as you?"

She rolled her eyes and turned to the side to ignore me.

"The next person to say something will be going to the office.", said the teacher.

They all started looking around at each other, but they stopped bullying for a minute. When recess came, students cleared their desks and started for the playground. The teacher stood outside of the door until she thought the room was clear. As she was closing the door behind her, she was startled to look up and see me still sitting in my desk.

"Cole, why are you still in here?"

"I didn't want to go outside."

"Are you sick?"

"No ma'am."

"You can't stay in here, go outside and get some fresh air".

"Do I have to?"

"Yes.", she stated without a smile.

I got up and did as she told me to and I hated it. Once again, the kids made fun of me. Boys were running over my feet and I was so mad till I finally lashed out. The Little class smarty pants (Who I quickly figured out was the teacher's pet), ran across my feet and just as he passed me, I took my fist and whacked him in the back, right at the time, Mrs. Williams came through the door to peek out at the class just in time to see me hit Lennard in his back. He arched his back and yelled out in pain. *"Both of you come here right now!"*

He ran over to her with tears streaming, now I was shaking like a leaf.

"Come to my room, both of you! Right now!", she had her hand on his back, and gave me a soft push through the door. When we got into the room she sat at the end of the desk.

"Cole, you just got here…"

"*But he started it!!* "

"*Be quiet and listen. We do not hit or fight our classmates! Do you understand?*"

"*Yes ma'am.*", I said as I was crying.

"*Lennard, what did you do?*"

"*I wus just praying wif her.*" He lied. (He had a speech problem).

"*You wasn't playin!*" I shot back.

"*Yes I wus!*"

"*No you weren't!*"

"*Yes I wus!*"

"*That's enough!*" Mrs. Williams said with a firm voice.

"*He was stepping...*"

"*I said that's enough, Cole.*"

"*But he was...*"

"*I said that's enough Cole*"!

"*He was...*"

"*I said be quiet!*"

"*Stepping on my foot!*", I said very quickly. I just had to get it out.

"*Both of you go to your seats. You'll spend the remainder of recess inside.*"

I noticed that she glanced down at my shoes, but she didn't say anything at first. Then she called Lennard back. "*Lennard come here.*" He had the back of his hand up to his mouth as he slowly walked to her desk. She stood up and escorted him to the hallway. I could see them because she had not closed the door completely. Her arms were folded as she looked down at him. He was looking downward and slowly shaking his head. I could hear their voices, but I couldn't understand what they were saying.

When they came back inside, seems like he was coming my way.

As he slowly walked, he turned to look at Mrs. Williams. With the slightest of a smile she said, *"Go on."*
He gave a large sigh, came over towards me with his hands jammed down in his pockets and mumbled out, *"Shorry."*
"Cole, tell him you're sorry."
I'm wondering to myself, *"Why should I say I'm sorry? I didn't do nothin'."*
I was looking at him, and he was looking at me.
I sighed a deep sigh and whispered,
"Me too."
I was too proud to say I'm sorry, but so was he. Lennard snatched away from my desk complaining about how I made him sick. I put my head down on my desk to finish crying.
"Cole.", said Mrs. Williams. *"Why are you crying?"*
"I don't know."
"Go wash your face and finish recess... you too, Lennard."
We left out of the room separately. I went outside and started playing alone.
Lennard went over to the guys in class. I don't know what he was saying to them,
but they laughed when they were near me, but they did not bother me anymore.
There was another girl from the class who seemed to be a loner. She was pushing a merry-go-round and then she would hop on it. When it slowed down, she jumped off and push again, I ran over to help and we both started pushing . Then we would hold our heads back and squeal with delight. Now my day was about to make a wonderful turn. As we were walking back towards class we started to talk.
"What's your name?", I asked her.
"Evelyn.", she said.
"What's yours?"

"Debora.", I said.
"Wanna do it again next recess?"
"Yeah."
We became the best of friends and here we are 55 yrs. later. Still friends. Anyway, Evelyn was one of the reason I looked forward to going to school. She was an outsider like me. They would tease her because she was small. Her feet did not touch the floor as she sat in her desk. I guess they didn't go too far because she was smart. As the days go by, the bullying began to become less and less. I guess the kids were ready to move on to another victim. Bullying me was getting boring, I guess.

Now we were at a time in the year when all students would have to take the standardized tests. We used to call them the dot test. The tests were to be taken over a period of three days. Normal work would resume after the testing came to an end. Little did I know this testing period would be my opening door for acceptance. The next Monday, when everyone had settled in that morning, Mrs. Williams walked in and she seemed somewhat happy-dry, but happy.
"Good morning, class.", she said.
"Good morning, Mrs. Williams.", everyone said.
She walked around to the front of her desk and leaned on it before she
Begin to speak. All our eyes were anxiously waiting to hear what she had to say.
"Children, it is time for us to have our testing period. Monday, Tuesday, and Wednesday of next week."
"What is a testing period?", asked a student.
"There will be 3 days of test that all students must take."

She passed out a sheet to everyone. *"Give these to your parents so they can help you to be at your best."*
The sheet basically said to go to bed at a reasonable time, get a good night's sleep, have a good breakfast. Then Mr. Smarty Pants, Lennard just had to open his mouth. First he raised his hand, scrambled out of his seat and begin to talk. Remember now, he had a speech problem. *"Mish Weoms."*, he begin. *"You know I Prowly gon' Pash dat tesh. My Momma finna put me in the fiff grade. Sho dis tesh gon be eshy."* Lennard was about 4 feet tall with a big head, he had on a plaid shirt with suspenders to hold up his pants, which by the way, had large cuffs because he was so short. *"Aint no tesh too hard for me!"*

He said as he pointed to himself. Then he folded his arms and grinned. Everyone laughed because he had a few teeth missing, but it didn't matter to him. Even grouchy Mrs. Williams laughed.
"Lennard, would you please sit back down?"
"Yesh Ma'am", he said.
Then he scrambled back into his seat. He was a little boy with a big ego.
They all giggled.
"Don't forget now class.", said Mrs. Williams. *"Give this to your mother or daddy so they can help you to prepare for your tests."*
"Yes ma'am.", we said in unison.
"Make sure that you place that announcement into your satchel so you won't forget and leave it in your desk."
"Yes ma'am.", we all replied.
There was much rustling and bumping around and chatter as we did what we were told to do. The kids in the So-called smart group chattered excitedly, while the kids in the remedial group was slowly

fumbling with their announcement and carelessly jamming it into their satchels and whatever they had to carry their school supplies. Some of them just stuffed it into their desks. One girl sat at her desk with her lip poked out and just let it fall to the floor. That proved to be the wrong thing to do.

"Hattie, pick that paper up!", said the teacher.

Hattie propped her face on her hand, and continued to stare down. Comparing her to the rest of us, she was a large sized child. I didn't know if she was older or just big for her age, but one thing for sure, I wasn't going to ask her. I felt kinda sorry for her because no one ever talked to her.

"Hattie, did you hear me?"

Hattie just continued to look down as she flipped her pencil end to end.

"Hattie!"

No response.

"Hattie Lewis!"

Hattie took a big sigh without ever looking up.

"What!", she shouted.

Everyone stopped whatever they were doing, and started staring at Hattie. When the teacher walked over to her we all watched anxiously to see what was going to happen. She walked up to Hattie with a 12-inch ruler in her hand.

"Oh no!" I thought to myself. *"She's gonna hit her! Pick it up, Hattie. Please pick it up!"*

But Hattie's pride sat in. She reminded me of myself. People picked on her because of her size, plus, she had an odor. I could only bow my head. I knew what she was going through.

"Pick up your paper, Hattie.", said the teacher as she tapped her own hand with the ruler. Still no response from Hattie. Suddenly we heard something like a slap. She had whacked Hattie across her shoulder

with the ruler. Hattie didn't budge, but you could see the tears falling from her eyes onto her desk.

"Hattie pick up the paper!"

Still didn't budge.

After 2 or 3 more times, Hattie still didn't pick it up. I felt bad for Hattie. A few tears fell from my eyes.

Finally, the teacher got tired of hitting Hattie and told her to go to the office. Right before she left, teacher wrote a note and gave it to Hattie. She snatched the note from the desk and went to the office. Everyone was whispering. Some of them were giggling. Nothing was funny to me. One thing I did see, was that teacher did not have a heart.

Hattie came back into the class still looking the same way she did when she left out. She placed a note on the teacher's desk without looking at her, went back to her seat and resumed her position. She picked up her pencil and once again resumed flipping her pencil end to end.

"Hattie, you won't have recess this morning.", said the teacher.

"So."

"Your mouth is going to get you in trouble, young lady!"

Hattie just humped her shoulders as if she didn't care. Teacher just stared at her, but Hattie never looked up. Out of the blue, she leaned over, picked up the announcement from the floor, dusted it off and placed it in her satchel. Unless I'm imagining things, she seemed to have a slight smile and a smirk on her face.

After that incident, the remainder of the day seemed to go along pretty smoothly. For me, an occasional sneer from someone, being called ugly black girl, or insult of some kind, had become a common everyday thing, so it didn't bother me too much anymore.

Evelyn and I had become the best of buddies now. We played together every recess. Sometimes we seem to be having such a good time that others join in with us. Today as we sat on the see-saw we discussed the upcoming test.

"*I hope this test is not too hard.*", Evelyn said.

"*Me too.*", I said.

"*I hope this test is not too hard.*", Evelyn said.

"*Me too.*", I said.

"*Why do they want us to eat breakfast?*"

"*Don't know. I guess so we can think better.*"

"*Why do they want us to go to bed early?*"

"*So we don't go to sleep, I guess.*"

"*Humm.*", said Evelyn.

"*I don't wanna talk about the test anymore. Have you ever played Bump on the seesaw?*", I asked her.

"*What's bump?*", she asked.

"*I'll show you.*", I said.

I explained the game to her. She looked a little doubtful. (I know it was because of her size). We both were rather small, so I didn't think it would hurt either one of us. I asked Evelyn,

"*Ready to try it?*"

"*Yeah. I guess.*"

"*Hold on tight.*"

Not only did she hold on tight, she closed her eyes tightly. I went up, and when I came down, I pushed the see-saw down hard. Her whole body flew into the air, but she held on. I was impressed! When she came down I flew into the air. That was a fun time for us. As we bumped, others came and started to look on. I started to hear the conversations of some of the others as they looked on.

"That looks stupid!"
"Old country girl do stupid stuff."
"I think I want to try that."
"Me too."

Pretty soon the other see-saw was being used by other kids who wanted to play "Bump". They didn't want to give up the see-saw. Believe it or not it was the ones who said the game looked stupid. The game went over so well that long lines of kids wanted to play. The playground teachers saw the long lines and came over to see what was going on. Our fun came to a halt when they saw how the game was played. We had to stop playing "Bump" because they said it was too dangerous. We hated that. As for Evelyn and me, it didn't stop us from having fun. We had big imaginations and could have fun in lots of ways.

The day arrived for the start of the standardized testing. It became the "Dot" Test to us because it was multiple choice, and we had to darken one of the dots for the chosen answer. That night before the tests begin, my cousins, my sister and I were very cooperative at bedtime because we were anxious about what was to come. Going to bed still didn't work for me because I was too anxious to sleep. I tossed and turned and wrinkled the sheets. I moved around so much that night, that when morning came I was so exhausted! I nodded off into my cereal.

"Dep!!", my Sister exclaimed, as she shook my shoulder. Everyone was laughing at me, but I didn't think it was funny.

"What y'all laughing at!"

"You!!" They all said in unison.

My mother said, *"Go wash your face."*

"I already washed my face!"

"Do it again so you can wake up !!"

I was feeling pretty cranky that morning. I was supposed to get a good night's sleep and I didn't. I was supposed to eat breakfast, not sleep in it. I was supposed to eat breakfast, not sleep in it. Even Rodney and Nita didn't bother me that morning. I must have looked pretty rough.

Nita only sneered and said, *"Yuck."*

I didn't even care. As we got closer to the school, I became more and more alert. I knew I had to be alert when I got to my class room. Kids seemed more chatty and lively than usual, or was it me being more tired than usual. When I reached my class the first face I looked into was none other than Lennard He had about ten fancy-looking pencils on his desk then it hit me like a brick! I forgot all about the pencils!! I panicked.

Desk by painful desk, humiliating, piercing eyes, nasty sneers, snake flicking tongues, horrible nose crinkles, sighs of disgust, eyes rolling. I thought I had finally gotten past this part of the mean-spirited, spitefulness of the classmates. Can you imagine, having to stand before the desk of each and every one of them to beg for a pencil, only to be turned away? As I walk away, I hear mumbles or sniggles. After about the tenth person, I stopped in my tracks and turned to the teacher without saying a word, my face should have told the story. Her steel-cold black eyes looked at me without a snippet of sympathy. She sat at her desk leaning back in her chair, with her arms folded without a blink or wink.

"Hurry up Cole! We need to start this test in five minutes!"

I continued on my quest for this stupid pencil until I could not hold The tears any longer. Finally, of all people, Lennard; who had about ten pencils of different sizes, shapes, and colors, decided he would let me use a regular yellow, chewed up pencil with almost no eraser. I think I stood in front of him about 30 seconds before the words would come out of my mouth. I said in an almost whisper, *"May I borrow a pencil?"*

I could tell he didn't want to. But He let me use the old pencil. He looked at me like he was silently saying, *"You better give it back."*

After being humiliated for what seemed forever, I finally returned back to my seat, embarrassed, belittled, hurt...but never defeated. I could see from the corners of my eyes that all were watching me. I was so angry. Tired of being bullied, talked about, and treated like I was nothing. This was the moment I decided that I was going to show them that I was no dummy. I was smart and I knew it. I may not have been a super genius like Lennard, but I was above my peers. They thought I was stupid, and I thought they were stupid. But I made up in my mind that I was going to prove to them that I was not stupid, dumb or whatever they called me. I dried up those tears and sat up straight in my seat with determination. I had a point to prove.

"Cole, did you say thank you?"

"Naw, she didn't.", interrupted Lennard. *"Thanks."*, I flatly stated.

"Turn to him and say it.", she demanded.

"Thanks."

"Wasting test time", she muttered.

"Turn your tests over." She gave us a little explanation of what we were to do.

We already understood about multiple choice—well, most of us. The remedial needed a little more instruction from the teacher. I finished my first test quickly. As usual she had a frown on her face, when she looked at me and said, *"Cole, you need to be doing your test, not daydreaming."*

I looked at her with my head held high with a renewed confidence and just like her, flatly stated, *"I finished already."*

For once, I saw a difference on her face. One eyebrow went up. All kids Stopped and looked at me. Lennard slammed his pencil down because He did not finish first.

"You need to look over your answers, Cole."

"I already looked over my answers!"

"Look again! You may have some of them wrong!"

The test was a reading test. Little did she know that I had won Certificates, prizes and awards and gifts because I was the best reader in the school from where I came I loved reading!! On that particular test, we found out a couple of days later that I made one hundred.

Anyway, the testing continued until Thursday. On Friday, they gave us a break after the week of testing. My friend Evelyn and I had a good day of not being bothered or meddled by anyone. We saw where the kids had resumed playing "Bump" on the seesaw and nobody tried to stop them. The week ended on a good note. When the evening came and I got on the bus to go home, Rodney and Nita happened to be sitting in a seat across from where I was. I was hoping that they would not say a word to me. They were a grade below me, and they were always teaming up together when they were bullying people. I couldn't believe it when Nita asked me, "Hey girl, what yo' name?"

"Debora.", I said.

That was the end of that conversation and bullying from them. I was thinking to myself, *"Wow!"*

I wondered if someone had told on them or they just got tired of me and needed a new target. I didn't care. Now I could ride the bus in peace. After that week of testing, things came back to normal. No more eight o' clock bedtimes, no more breakfast if we didn't want it and best of all, no more regular bullying. Every now and then someone might throw in a small insult. I had become so used to being the laughing stock and the butt of everyone's jokes that I thought something was wrong with the people who didn't do it anymore.

I know that everyone was happier now that the testing was over. They seemed to be more playful and just a tad bit more friendlier. The teachers seemed to be more relaxed and not as grumpy. We begin to get into our regular routine and after about 3 or 4 days, the taunting and teasing started again, but not as much, though. Maybe they were concerned as to whether they passed the test or not. We did not understand that. It was a test to find out about your learning skills. Everyone was chattering nervously about it because nobody wanted to *"flunk"* and get left behind.

Finally, the day came when our test scores were returned. Mrs. Williams tapped on her desk with her ruler to get everyone's attention.

"Good Morning," she said.

"Good morning, Mrs. Williams."

"As you all can see, Lennard's seat is empty".

According to them, He had never missed a day before.

"Well where is he?" Asked his friend Kevin.

"He ain't dead is he?" Asked Frank, with a toothy smile.

"Boy! Naw he ain't dead!!" Exclaimed Robert.

"Is he Mrs. Williams?"

She looked upwards as she took a deep breath and looked at the boys with squinted eyes.

"No he is not dead?"

"Well where he at?" Asked Larry.

"Nona yo' business!!" Said Lee.

"Boys! Boys! Shhhhhhh!!!" Warned Mrs. Williams.

"Give me a chance and I'll tell you all."

I looked at her in surprise.

'*Whhhaaattt*" I thought to myself. "*She can smile!*"
"*I thought her face was broke!*"
"*As I was about to say, children* ", said Mrs. Williams, "*Lennard has been promoted again, and he's been moved to another school.*"
The class begin once again to chatter. When they saw names being written on the board they became very nervous. When I saw that my name was the third name on the list, I could feel my heart thumping It must not have been too bad, because Lennard's name was first, Lee's was next and then mine. When the teacher stopped writing, She slowly looked at everyone and then she zeroed in on me. She only put five names on the board.
"Class", she began, "*These students scored the top five grades in the third grade.*"
There were gasps, oohs and ahs mouth-over-hand but mostly stares At me! Yes! me! The skinny little bumpkin from Slot Pot! I was happy, but it was no surprise to me. I expected to do well.
"Cole", get your things out of your desk and come sit here."
 More mumbling and chattering. All eyes watched me as I moved to my new seat.
"*I didn't know she was that smart!*"
"*Hummm, but you still ugly!*"
The girl who said that, laughed alone. She didn't get the response that She thought she would. One of the boys said,
"*You need to shut up with your big mouth*".
Everyone laughed at her, and the teacher had to call back the class to order.to order.
Hard in my chest. Then the teacher spoke and said,
"Cole, this is your seat from now on".
"Yes Ma'am,"
"*What do you think about me now?*" I thought to myself.
By the look on her face, she still could not believe that

I passed that test. Neither could half of the students, but It didn't matter. All I know is that I proved my point. I wanted everyone—especially Mrs. Williams—not to judge me by what I looked like or where I came from. Just treat me like a normal 3rd grader. That's all.

www.ingramcontent.com/pod-product-compliance
Lightning Source LLC
LaVergne TN
LVHW021050100526
838202LV00082B/5429